Christmas Coloring

Copyright ©2017 Tabitha L. Barnett

This publication is protected by copyright law. Please respect the law. No part of this publication can be reproduced, reused, republished, or stored in a database or retrieval system without prior written consent from the artist. The one exception to this policy is that you are premitted to photocopy the original pages in this book to color for your own personal use.

Christmas Circles
©2017 Tabitha L Barnett
ISBN-13: 978-1979637619
ISBN-10: 197963761X

©2017 Tabitha Barnett

©2017 Tabitha Barnett

©2017 Tabitha Barnett

©2017 Tabitha Barnett

Santa's Workshop

©2017 Tabitha Barnett

©2017 Tabitha Barnett

©2017 Tabitha Barnett

©2017 Tabitha Barnett

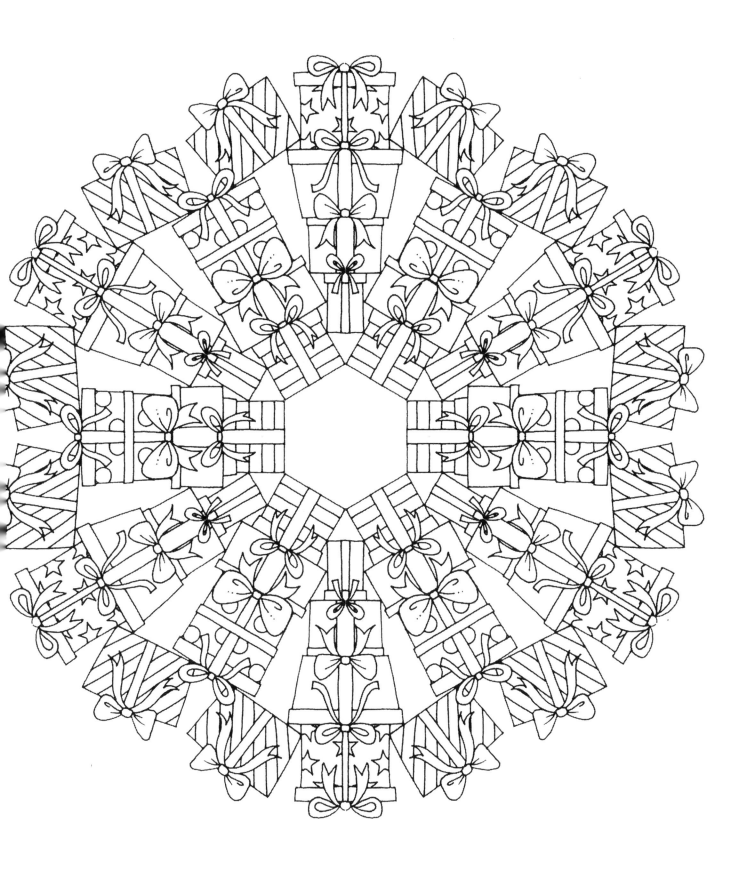

©2017 Tabitha Barnett

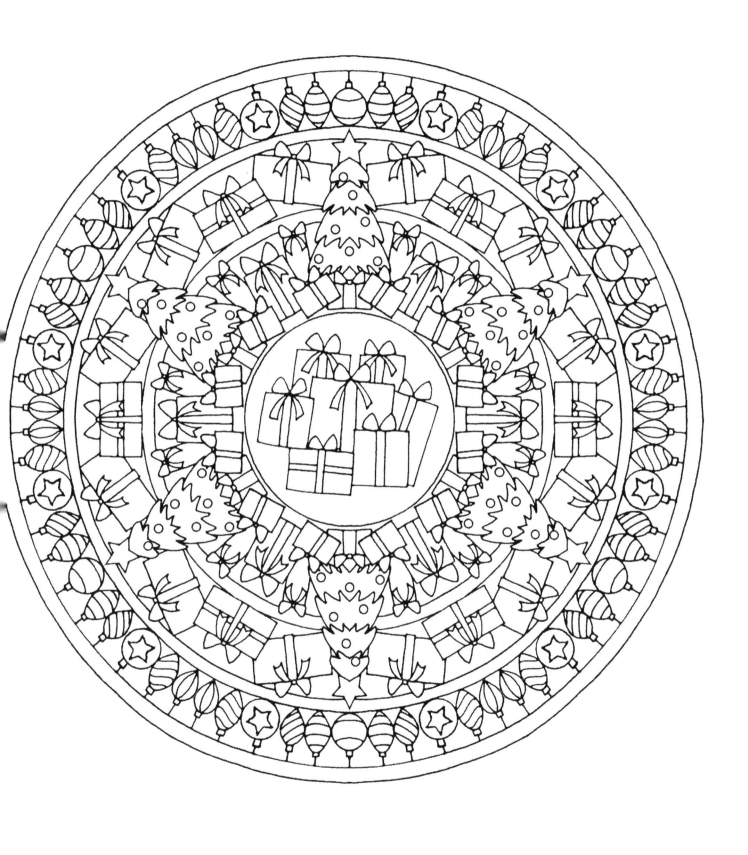
©2017 Tabitha Barnett

©2017 Tabitha Barnett

©2017 Tabitha Barnett

©2017 Tabitha Barnett

©2017 Tabitha Barnett

©2017 Tabitha Barnett

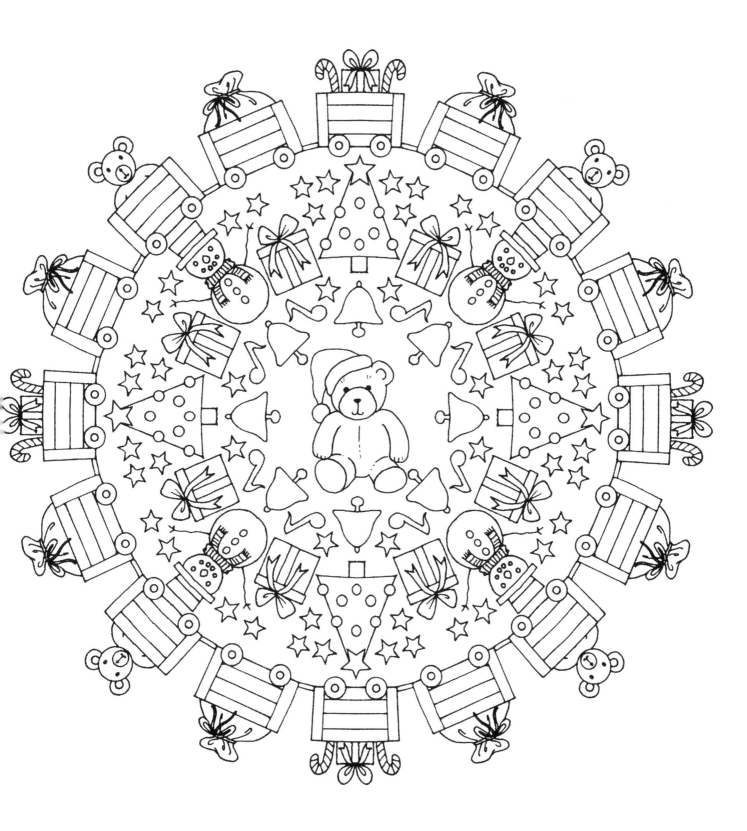

©2017 Tabitha Barnett

©2017 Tabitha Barnett

©2017 Tabitha Barnett

©2017 Tabitha Barnett

Join the conversation on facebook:
www.facebook.com/tabbystangledart

If you enjoyed this book, please consider taking a few minutes to leave a review on Amazon.

Please post your colored images online with
#tabbystangledart or #tabbyb so I can find them easily.

Instagram: @tabbystangledart
Twitter: @tabbyleann
www.patreon.com/tabbyb
www.sellfy.com/tabbyb
www.redbubble.com/people/tabbyb
www.amazon.com/author/tabbystangledart
http://tinyurl.com/tabbytube

Made in the USA
Middletown, DE
16 November 2017